Sevinchoy Mamatsoliyeva

The poetic world of Alexander Feinberg

Sevinchoy Mamatsoliyeva

The poetic world of Alexander Feinberg

The eternal echo of words Alexander Faynberg's poetry of time and memeory

JustFiction Edition

Imprint

Any brand names and product names mentioned in this book are subject to trademark, brand or patent protection and are trademarks or registered trademarks of their respective holders. The use of brand names, product names, common names, trade names, product descriptions etc. even without a particular marking in this work is in no way to be construed to mean that such names may be regarded as unrestricted in respect of trademark and brand protection legislation and could thus be used by anyone.

Cover image: www.ingimage.com

Publisher:
JustFiction! Edition
is a trademark of
Dodo Books Indian Ocean Ltd. and OmniScriptum S.R.L publishing group

120 High Road, East Finchley, London, N2 9ED, United Kingdom
Str. Armeneasca 28/1, office 1, Chisinau MD-2012, Republic of Moldova, Europe
Managing Directors: Ieva Konstantinova, Victoria Ursu
info@omniscriptum.com

Printed at: see last page
ISBN: 978-620-0-10679-7

The poetic world of Alexander Feinberg

The eternal echo of words Alexander Faynberg's poetry of time and memeory

Alexander Feinberg: The World of His Poetry

Alexander Feinberg's poetry is a reflection of time, memory, and the deep emotions that define human existence. His verses are filled with **melancholy, nostalgia, and the beauty of fleeting moments,** capturing the essence of love, solitude, and unspoken words.

His poems, such as *Snow Flowers*, *Sheet,* and *Moonlight,* transport readers into a world where **snow burns the lips, torn pages protect poetry, and stars hang from a fisherman's net**. Each piece carries a quiet depth, exploring the struggles of the soul and the search for meaning in an ever-changing world.

Feinberg's poetry is not just about words—it is about the **echo they leave behind**. His works remind us that poetry is a bridge between the past and the present, between sorrow and hope. He writes about **words that arrive too late**, about **the vastness of nature**, and about **the restless human spirit that seeks truth and peace.**

Through his **vivid imagery and heartfelt emotions**, Feinberg creates a poetic universe where every verse is a whisper from the past, resonating through time. His legacy lives on in the hearts of those who find meaning in his words.

SNOW FLOWERS

January in Moscow.

A storm is roaring underground.

Where to, my love?

Central telegraph. On each staircase,

frozen frost is blue.

I walk through them, leader -

a city full of people.

January snow burns your lips,

It hits the street lamps and flies through the subway.

You are not there - you are everywhere.

My love is mine. My last love.

Suvorov Avenue.

A pile of snow.

My heart gasps from the flight.

I see -

You are heading for the Arbat, my youth.

The hem of your coat is pulled by

The snow is falling - falling.

QOR UCHQUNLARI

Moskvada yanvar.
Bo'ron jaranglaydi yerosti bo'ylab.
Qayoqqa, sevgim?
Markaziy telegraf. Har bir zinada
qotib qolgan ayoz moviyrang.
Ularni oralab
chiqaman peshvoz –
odam to'la shahar.

Yanvar qori labni kuydirar,
Fonuslarga urilib chirs – chirs,
erosti yo'lidan o'tadi uchib.
Sen u yerda yo'qsan –
hammayoqdasan.
Sevgim mening. Eng so'nggi sevgim.
Suvorov hiyoboni.
Qorlar uyumi.
Yurak hapqiradi parvozdan.
Ko'rayapman –
Arbatga yo'l olding, yoshligim.
Tortqilaydi paltong etaklarini
Sochilib – sochilib ketayotgan qor.

Explanation of the poem "Snow Flowers"

This poem is a philosophical reflection on love, loss, and memories through the winter landscape of Moscow. The poet combines natural phenomena with emotions, expressing his inner experiences through unique images.

The first line of the poem - "January in Moscow" - not only indicates the place and time of the events, but also gives an emotional description of the cold, snowy winter season. The Moscow winter is not just a background, but is closely connected with the poet's mood and inner experiences. While a storm is raging underground, love, like this storm, shakes the heart. The poet, as if searching for his beloved, asks "Where to, my love?" - that is, "Where to, my beloved?" This sentence strongly reflects the feeling of loss and search.

In the next stanza, the poet describes the central telecommunications building in Moscow, the stairs covered with snow, and feels the city environment covered with a bitter cold. He is walking through the city, but this time he is walking not only physically, but also in his heart. The city is crowded, but he is lonely. This contrast reveals the inner emptiness of a person in the city environment.

One of the most touching lines of the poem is "January snow burns your lips." Although snow is usually felt as cold, here it is described as hot, burning. This symbolizes the bitterness and sweetness of love, the painful effect of loss. Snow "burns" not only the lips, but also the heart. The poet does not have a lover, but he is everywhere - this reflects the feeling that cannot be erased from the heart even after losing a loved one.

The last part of the poem depicts the snowdrifts on Suvorov Avenue, the poet's heart suffocating from flight, his youth walking towards the Arbat. These images are full of longing for the past years of youth and the feeling that they will not return. The poet's lover is probably not just a person - it can also be his youthful love, memories or lost dreams.

Summary:

The poem "Snow Flowers" is a deeply philosophical meditation on love, memory, and loss, depicting the inner suffering of the human soul through the bitter cold of a Moscow winter. The poet's love for his beloved is eternal, but this love lives on in memories. The poem reminds us that some things change over time, but memories held in the heart never fade.

SPACIOUS

What beautiful fields! The taste of the grass!

In my mother's footsteps - the pain is shameless.

My life now passes on my knees

Before my mother's life forever.

Block is this, the height. An incomparable poet.

In fact, we - earthlings - have a different fate.

They call it literature. This is also a mystery to me,

We cannot find happiness, there is no peace for us.

We dream on the right - hypocrisy and love,

Face - the hooves of battles that kick in the eye.

The struggle is endless. The feeling that cannot be separated from you -

When I can't see peace even in a dream.

KENGLIK

Na go'zal dalalar! Maysalar toti!
Onam izlarida – og'riq beadad.
Tiz cho'kib o'tadi endi hayotim
Onamning hayoti oldida abad.

***

Blok – bu, yuksaklik. Beqiyos shoir.
Asli, biz – yerliklar taqdiri o'zga.
Adabiyat derlar. Bu ham menga sir,
Halovat topilmas, huzur yo'q bizga.

O'ngda tush ko'ramiz – riyo va sevgi,
Yuz – ko'zga tepinar janglar tuyog'i.
Kurash tinmas. Sendan ayrilmas sezgi –
Oromni tushda ham ko'rmayman chog'i.

Explanation of the poem "Spacious"

This poem describes the pain of the human psyche, the image of the mother, the contradictions in literature and life. In a deeply philosophical and emotionally charged tone, the poet illuminates the complexity of the world, the gap between literature and reality.

The first stanza of the poem begins with a description of nature: "What beautiful fields! The taste of the grass!" These lines remind of the innocence of childhood, harmony with nature. But in the following verses, a painful contrast arises: following in the footsteps of the mother becomes painful and unforgivable. Here the poet connects the fate of the mother with his own life - her life is spent on her knees, while the mother's life is destined for eternity. These verses reflect the complexity of human life, the spiritual connection and selflessness between mother and child.

The next stanza talks about the great figure of Russian literature - Alexander Blok. The poet calls him "an incomparable poet", but notes that we - ordinary people - experience a completely different fate. For the poet, literature is a mystery, a riddle. He seeks to understand the true essence of literature, but does not find peace and happiness there either. These lines show the difference between art and life: literature cannot respond to a person's spiritual quest, it only opens up another mysterious world.

The third stanza is about the inner suffering of humanity, hostility and the inability to find peace. The poet emphasizes that the struggle in life is eternal, our dreams are caught between two opposing forces - "hypocrisy and love". The last lines are about the inability to see peace even in dreams. This expresses the inner suffering of humanity, the endless social and personal struggles.

Summary :

The poem "Spacious" is a deeply philosophical reflection on life, literature and human suffering. Although the poet reflects nature and childhood through vivid images, the complexity of life and the inner pain of man remain the primary theme. Literature is a riddle, and life is a constant struggle in which peace and happiness cannot be found. The poem retains a sense of heaviness and relentless search in the human spiritual world until the end.

MOONLIGHT

Standing on the edge of the night sky
A fisherman thinks silently, alone.
A net of bows on his shoulders,
Everything shines in the moonlight.

Stars hang from the net,
A silver boat, handfuls of gold.
The oars are buried in the light
The fine sands ripple.

OY MANZARASI

Tungi osmon chetida turib
Baliqchi jim, yolg'iz o'y surar.
Yelkasida yoyilar to'ri,
Oy nurida borliq yarqirar.

Osiladi yulduzlar to'rga,
Kumush qayiq, hovuch – hovuch zar.
Eshkaklarni ko'mgancha nurga
Mavjlanadi parsimon qumlar.

Explanation of the poem "Moonlight"

This poem is rich in metaphors, reflecting loneliness, a quiet night and the mysterious beauty of life. The poet illuminates the inner world of man through images of nature.

The poem begins with the image of a fisherman standing alone on the edge of the evening sky. This image expresses a person's lonely thoughts, life reflections and harmony with nature. The fisherman is silent, he is alone, but this loneliness does not oppress the heart - on the contrary, there is a calmness in him. The poet describes him with the phrase "A net of bows on his shoulders". This phrase can symbolize the complexity of life or the spiritual burden on a person's shoulders.

In the next lines of the poem, the stars in the sky are described as hanging from the fisherman's net. This image evokes feelings of both beauty and wonder. The lines "A silver boat, handfuls of gold" refer to the mysterious radiance of nature. Here, the boat may be shining in the moonlight, and the gold is the play of starlight or reflected light falling on the water.

The poem ends with the words "The oars are buried in the light, The fine sands ripple." This image blurs the line between reality and fantasy, as if the fisherman is standing between the real world and a mysterious, magical world.

Summary:

The poem "Moonlight" creates a mysterious and poetic landscape. Through the images of moonlight, stars, and water, the poet illuminates the subtle beauty of nature, the mystery of life, and the innermost feelings of man. The fisherman is not just a man fishing, but a symbolic figure who thinks deeply about life and lives in harmony with nature. The poem takes the reader into a world of tranquility and dreams, introducing him to beauty and philosophy.

Meeting

Let's promise to meet,

It's not a sin to meet.

Let's go somewhere,

Away from people's eyes.

Guitar and violin accompany,

Slowly the melody plays.

Whatever you wish, waitress,

The moon will be ready in an instant.

Snow-like foams dance and play

The time when champagne is opened.

Life seems carefree,

As if it were a dream.

Wine washes away sorrow from the heart,

Folding its wings softly,

Love and trust both

Slowly sit next to us.

Trust alone, love alone

We can't talk honestly.

We both have everything,

Only hope is missing.

Uchrashuv

Uchrashuvga va'dalashaylik,
Uchrashmoqlik emas-ku gunoh.
Qaygadir bosh olib ketaylik,
Odamlarning ko'zidan uzoq.

Gitara va skripka jo'r,
Sekingina taralar navo.
Ne tilasang, ofitsiant momo
Bir lahzada aylar muhayyo.

Sachrab o'ynar qordek ko'piklar
Shampan-sharob ochilgan zamon.
Betashvishdek tuyular hayot,
Bo'lmagandek go'yoki armon.

Sharob g'amni yuvar ko'ngildan,
Qanotlarin yig'ib ohista,
Muhabbat va ishonch ikkovlon
Yonimizga o'ltirar asta.

Ishonch birla, muhabbat birla
Suhbatlasha olmaymiz ro'yrost.
Ikkimizda hamma narsa bor,
Faqatgina umid yo'q, xolos.

Explanation of the poem "Meeting"

This poem is written in a romantic and melancholic spirit, and embodies the themes of meeting, love and hope. The poet skillfully uses musical and visual details to describe human feelings.

The poem begins with an invitation: "Let's promise to meet" - "Let's promise to meet." Although this is a simple proposal, it has a deep meaning - meeting is not just an action, but a sign of an inner need, a desire for intimacy. The following lines describe the meeting taking place in a mysterious environment: "Away from people's eyes" - "Away from people's eyes." This shows that intimacy should be felt only by the hearts of two people.

The presence of music is felt throughout the poem: "Guitar and violin accompany, Slowly the melody plays." The melodies of the guitar and violin add tenderness and charm to the meeting. This image is intertwined with love and beauty in life.

The next lines describe the moment when the champagne is opened. "Life seems carefree, As if it were a dream" – "Life seems like a dream, a silent dream." These lines express the magic of the moment – as if life is free from worries for a moment. But this is only a temporary state, at the end of the poem the true suffering of the human heart is clearly revealed.

In the last lines, the poet reaches the deepest layers of emotions: "We both have everything, Only hope is missing." – "We both have everything, Only hope is missing." This is the most difficult, but also the most truthful part of the poem. Although the poet feels love, trust, the beauty of the moment, the lack of faith in the future is revealed as a painful truth.

Summary :

The poem "Meeting" describes a romantic meeting, but also illuminates the subtle suffering of the human heart. The poem strongly contrasts the momentary happiness and eternal despair. The meeting is as beautiful as a fairy tale, as a dream, but it still contains a deep sense of loneliness and inadequacy. The poet describes the feelings in a very subtle and poetic way, which makes the poem touching and unforgettable for the reader.

Word

A train is late,

The eye is thirsty waiting for the plane.

The real misfortune, the great tragedy is

If it is late, the word that is expected.

As regretful as when standing over an extinguished bonfire,

As sad as when looking at a deserted hut

A late word is strange and cries badly,

For the people who waited for it yesterday.

Because of a late word, the forests are orphaned,

The foreheads of the vast lands are salty.

Even words are silent and silent near the graves,

Souls are restless and fate is blind.

So'z

Poezd kechikishi oddiy voqea,
Samolyotni kutib ichikadi ko'z.
Haqiqiy baxtsizlik, katta fojia –
Mabodo kechiksa kutilyotgan so'z.

So'ngan gulxan uzra bo'lgandek pushmon,
Kimsasiz kulbaga boqqandek mahzun
Kechikkan so'z g'arib, yig'laydi yomon,
Uni kecha kutgan odamlar uchun.

Kechikkan so'z bois o'rmonlar yetim,
Bepoyon yerlarning peshonasi sho'r.
Qabrlar qoshida so'z ham beso'z, jim,
Ruhlar bezovtayu qismat ko'zi ko'r.

Explanation of the poem "Word"

This poem philosophically and poetically describes the power of words, the consequences of their timely or delayed delivery. The poet says that the greatest misfortune in human life is the delay of the expected word, and describes the profound impact of this delay.

The first lines of the poem are reminiscent of a late train and an impatiently awaited plane. These images may refer to ordinary delays in life, but in the following lines the poet reveals the most severe form of such delays: the delay of the expected word. In life, it is important to say some words on time - if they are late, their value does not change, but rather causes pain.

In the following lines the poet emphasizes how sad a late word is: "A late word is strange and cries badly, For the people who waited for it yesterday." – "A late word cries strangely and bitterly, for those who waited for it yesterday." This line refers to the painful impact of words of regret, declaration of love, or forgiveness spoken late in a person's life.

The poet uses powerful metaphors to show that this delay affects even nature, such as the orphaning of forests and the salty foreheads of vast lands due to late words. The line "Even words are silent and silent near the graves" - "Even words are silent and silent near the graves" - shows that late words have no meaning when a person's life is over.

The last lines of the poem create a touching ending: "Souls are restless and fate is blind." - "Souls are restless and fate is blind." This probably means that the ghosts of people who died are restless because of untimely words, or that human fate is chaotic because of delays.

Summary :

The poem "Word" reminds us of the importance of timely words in human life. Words are a powerful weapon that must be used at the right time. If it is too late to say it, it will only bring regret, longing and suffering. The poet reveals this philosophy through real-life examples, powerful metaphors and poetic images. The poem invites the reader to deep reflection: the words that are not too late in life should be said now!

Sheet

The sky protects the stars,

The deep sea protects the mountains.

A sheet torn from my notebook,

Protect the poems I wrote.

Poetry is not only to read, to listen,

Poetry is a sound that resonates in the heart:

A path in the taiga as if saved,

A reed in the lakes as if swaying.

Every line of mine is a soul, every poem is a heart,

A hash to the forest, birds, clouds.

A sheet torn from my notebook,

Protect my poems, don't rush.

May the generations not be weary,

May my poems not be helpless,

May the wind, the sea and the leaves be like

Let them breathe, let them laugh innocently.

Varaq

Yulduzlarni asraydi falak,
Teran dengiz asrar durlarni.
Daftarimdan yirtilgan varaq,
Asragin men yozgan she'rlarni.

She'r – nafaqat o'qimoq, uqmoq,
She'r – yurakda yangragan tovush:
Qutqargandek taygada so'qmoq,
Tebrangandek ko'llarda qamish.

Har satrim – jon, har she'rim – yurak,
O'rmon, qushlar, bulutlarga xesh.
Daftarimdan yirtilgan varaq,
She'rlarimni asra peshma-pesh.

Avlodlarga kelmasin malol,
She'rlarim g'am chekmasin nochor,
Shamol, dengiz va yaproq misol
Nafas olsin, kulsin beg'ubor.

Explanation of the poem "Sheet"

This poem expresses the poet's creative heritage and love for poetry. Through poetic images, the poem explores the art of speech in the human soul, the importance of creativity, and its eternity over time.

From the very beginning, the poem is based on the concept of nature and protection. Just as the sky protects the stars and the sea protects the mountains, so a simple sheet of paper - the poet's drafts - protects his poems. Here it is emphasized that the poet's work, the lines from his heart, although written on ordinary paper, have infinite value in their essence.

The second stanza of the poem reveals the true essence of poetry. Poetry is not written just to read or listen, it is something that resonates in the human heart, affecting the soul. The poet compares poetry with life itself: like a road in the taiga salvation, as calm and charming as reeds on lakes. These similes show how closely the poet sees poetry as connected to life events.

In the next stanza, the poet connects his lines with the human soul and nature. Each line is a soul, and each poem is a heart. This indicates that poetry is not just words, but a force that reflects the inner world of a person. He describes his poems as an integral part of nature: as a work of art, harmoniously combined with the forest, birds and clouds. These lines symbolize the eternity of poetry - it is in harmony with nature, a living expression of human feelings.

The final part of the poem embodies the poet's hopes. He wishes that future generations will not get tired, that his poems will not be forgotten, that nature and creativity will be eternal. The wind, the sea and leaves - all this the poet wants to breathe in harmony with his poems and laugh as innocently as nature. This reflects the poet's faith in creativity, his desire to influence future generations through his lines.

Summary :

This poem reflects the poet's philosophical thoughts about creative heritage, the deep resonance of poetry in the human soul, and its harmony with nature. For the poet, each written line is not just simple words, but a spiritual experience from the heart, claiming eternity. This poem is a sincere and powerful work that proves that creativity is an eternal value.

DRAFT ODE

Poet, in this existence, dawn breaks,

Don't choose another path until the grave.

Be enchanted by the beauty of the earth, fall in love,

Sing with love, God is your helper.

However, poet, your white copies

Don't say they are all heartwarming, sparkling.

They will all surface one day.

Drafts that have been locked up for a lifetime

Like no one can be loyal to you.

In them - the blood, veins of your books,

They are creativity, courage, a burning guide.

They will bring you glory - fame,

Night drafts - like tears.

Drafts... seem ordinary, never

They do not betray - they do not forgive, but

After all, in this there are not words, letters,

The sound of a star that is not even visible to the eye.

Then – An invisible bond that reaches the truth,

Poet, preserve this bond, of course.

Poems can be memorized

But –

Moments are a unique sound.

Words, you don't rhyme, actually —

Blood brother – ini.

I wish you a flight high,

You can't burn without closing your eyes

Only, only a dra

QORALAMALAR QASIDASI

Shoir, shu borliqda tong chog'i ochil,
Boshqa yo'l tanlama qabrga qadar.
Yerning jamoliga maftun, oshiq bo'l,
Sevib – sevib kuyla, tangri madadkor.
Biroq,shoir, oqqa ko'chirmalaring
Bari ham diltortar, jilvagar dema.
Sirtga qalqib chiqar barisi bir kun.
Bir umr qulflangan qoralamalar
Kabi hech kim senga bo'lolmas sodiq.
Unda – kitoblaring qoni, tomiri,
U – ijod, jasorat, yo'lboshchi yoniq.
Ular olib kelar senga shon – shuhrat,
Tungi qoralama – ko'z yoshday egik.
Qoralama... oddiy ko'rinar, hech vaqt
Hiyonat qilmaslar – kechirmaslar lek
Axir, bunda so'zlar, harflar emas,
Ko'zga ham ilg'anmas yulduz tovushi.
Unda – Haqqa yetar ko'rinmas rishta,
Shoir, shu rishtani asra, albatta.
Yodlamoq mumkindir she'rlarni
Ammo –
Lahzalar betakror sado.
So'zlar, qofiyadosh emassiz,asli —
Qondosh og'a – ini.
Men parvoz tilayman sizlarga baland,
Ko'zni yummay turib yoqib bo'lmaydi
Faqat, faqat qoralamani.

Explanation of the poem "Ode to Drafts"

This poem is a philosophical observation about the poet's devotion to creativity and the importance of his drafts. The poem encourages the poet to wake up with the dawn, that is, to face a new day and new creativity. There is only one path for the poet - the path of creativity and art. Being fascinated by the beauty of the earth, loving it and singing this love is described as a divine duty for the poet.

However, one of the main ideas in the poem is that every written piece of paper, every draft is not an ordinary writing, but the heart, blood and veins of creativity. Although the poet strives to publish his books and poems, he understands that in fact his most faithful companions are his drafts. Because drafts never betray and never abandon the poet. They are the purest, most sincere part of creativity, the most intimate part of the human soul reflects deep feelings.

Another important aspect of the poem is its spiritual and philosophical layers. The poet does not consider the drafts to be a simple collection of words. They are the sound of the stars, that is, a divine melody that can only be heard with the heart. The poem uses the expression "an invisible bond," which means a divine connection with creation. The poet considers his creation to be connected not only to himself, but also to a higher power - God, and emphasizes the need to maintain this bond.

The last part of the poem has a very strong conclusion. The poet, while confirming the value of drafts, says that they cannot be burned. Because moments cannot be returned, each written line has its own voice and essence. One should only approach drafts without closing one's eyes, that is, consciously. This reflects the poet's respect and dedication to his work.

Summary :

This poem reflects the poet's devotion to creativity, the importance of drafts, and the divine power of the art of words. He views drafts not just as words on paper, but as deep suffering and feelings of the soul. This is a very deep and relevant topic for every creative person.

Conclusion

Alexander Feinberg's poetry is a timeless testament to the power of words and emotions. His verses, filled with **melancholy, nostalgia, and deep reflections**, capture the essence of human experience—**love, solitude, longing, and the passage of time**. Through his unique imagery, he transforms ordinary moments into something eternal, whether it be **snowfall in Moscow, a torn sheet preserving poetry, or a fisherman casting his net under the moonlight**.

His poetry serves as a bridge between **the past and the present, between memory and reality**, reminding us that words, once spoken or written, leave an indelible mark. Feinberg's work urges us to appreciate the beauty of fleeting moments and to express our thoughts before it is too late.

Though time moves forward, his poetry remains, echoing through generations. His words continue to inspire, to resonate, and to remind us that literature is not just an art—it is a way of preserving the soul's deepest truths. Through his legacy, Alexander Feinberg lives on, proving that poetry has the power to transcend time and touch the hearts of those who read it.

Alexander Feinberg was born in Tashkent in 1939. His name and work are dear to Uzbek readers and poetry lovers. More than ten collections of his poems have been published in Tashkent, Moscow and St. Petersburg. The scripts for seven feature films written by the poet are distinguished by their originality and vitality. He is the author of more than twenty cartoons and prose works. The interest of Uzbek readers in these works is also growing.

Alexander Feinberg is a remarkable poet whose literary contributions have left an indelible mark on Russian and Uzbek poetry. His works encapsulate a deep emotional intensity, blending personal experiences with broader societal themes. As a poet, Feinberg often navigates the complexities of human existence, freedom, and identity, offering readers profound insights into the struggles of his time. His poetry is distinguished by its lyrical depth, philosophical undertones, and evocative imagery, making him a unique voice in 20th-century literature.

Feinberg's poetry emerges from a historical and political context that profoundly shaped his worldview. Born during a tumultuous period in Soviet history, his writings reflect the conflicts between personal integrity and state-imposed ideologies. His verses often grapple with themes of resistance, exile, and the relentless pursuit of truth. Through a masterful use of language and metaphor, Feinberg conveys the inner turmoil of individuals who refuse to conform, highlighting the eternal struggle between the individual and authoritarian structures.

One of the defining features of Feinberg's poetry is his ability to capture raw human emotions with striking simplicity. His poems often carry an air of melancholy, yet they also exude resilience and an undying hope for justice and freedom. His use of rhythm and sound enhances the emotive power of his words, creating a melodic and almost hypnotic effect on the reader. This musicality, combined with his sharp wit and reflective tone, allows his poetry to transcend linguistic and cultural barriers.

Feinberg's works also exhibit a profound engagement with the themes of memory and exile. His poetry serves as both a personal and collective testimony, chronicling the pain of displacement and the longing for a lost homeland. He weaves together past and present, crafting verses that resonate with the experiences of those who have faced oppression and marginalization. His ability to transform suffering into art makes his poetry not only a form of resistance but also a beacon of hope.

Furthermore, Feinberg's poetic style is characterized by its rich inter textually and intellectual depth. He often draws inspiration from classical literature, philosophy, and historical events, infusing his work with multiple layers of meaning. His allusions to mythology, religious motifs, and existentialist themes provide a broader context for his reflections on human nature and society. This intellectual rigor, coupled with his passionate expression, makes his poetry both thought-provoking and deeply moving.

In conclusion, Alexander Feinberg's poetry stands as a testament to the enduring power of the written word. His ability to articulate the human condition with such depth and sincerity ensures that his works remain relevant across generations. His legacy is one of courage, truth, and poetic brilliance—an unwavering voice in the face of adversity. Whether exploring themes of exile, resistance, or personal introspection, Feinberg's poetry continues to inspire and challenge readers worldwide, offering a poignant reflection on the complexities of life and history.

Alexander Feinberg's poetry is a symphony of emotions, thoughts, and deep reflections on life, time, and human destiny. His works are filled with vivid imagery, philosophical depth, and an unbreakable connection to nature, history, and the soul's inner struggles.

Feinberg's poetic style is characterized by a delicate balance between nostalgia and reality, between love and solitude. His verses often explore the fleeting nature of time, the weight of unspoken words, and the power of human memory. Whether he writes about the vastness of the Russian winter, the loneliness of an abandoned word, or the quiet beauty of moonlight, his poetry carries a universal message that transcends borders and generations.

One of the key themes in his poetry is the importance of words—how they shape our reality, bring comfort, or leave behind an unhealed wound when spoken too late. In **"Word"**, he masterfully portrays the tragedy of a delayed word, emphasizing how time can turn simple expressions into irreversible regrets. Similarly, in **"Snow Flowers"**, he captures the silent beauty of winter while weaving in personal emotions of longing and reminiscence.

Feinberg's poetic world is also deeply intertwined with nature. His verses breathe with the rhythm of the wind, the softness of falling snow, and the endless horizons of fields and lakes. In **"Moonlight"**, he transforms the night sky into a mystical stage where a lone fisherman casts his net of stars, blurring the lines between reality and dream.

His poetry does not merely describe the external world—it delves into the depths of human consciousness, exploring themes of love, trust, loss, and hope. **"Meeting"** speaks of fleeting moments of happiness, while **"Spacious"** reflects on the struggle of finding peace in an imperfect world.

Alexander Feinberg's poetry invites readers to pause, reflect, and feel the weight of each word. It is a testament to the timeless power of language and the enduring beauty of emotions captured in verse. Through his works, he reminds us that words, like snowflakes, may seem delicate, but they hold the power to shape entire worlds.

Aleksandr Faynberg stands as a profound figure in literature, renowned for his intricate exploration of language, human emotions, and cultural identity. His works have significantly contributed to contemporary literary thought and sociolinguistic discussions. This article examines his literary legacy by analyzing his poetic works, with a particular focus on «Whispers of the Past.» Through this analysis, we will uncover his use of symbolism, stylistic devices, and thematic depth that define his unique artistic expression.

Born in St. Petersburg in 1952, Aleksandr Faynberg showed an early passion for literature and linguistics. He pursued formal education at Moscow State University, where he developed a keen interest in the interplay between language and cultural identity. Influenced by literary giants such as Boris Pasternak and Marina Tsvetaeva, he crafted his own distinctive literary style that blended philosophy with poetic expression. His early works reflected a deep interest in existentialism and the human condition, themes that would later define much of his poetry and essays.

Faynberg's works span multiple genres, but his poetry remains a cornerstone of his literary influence. His most renowned collections include Reflections in the Mist, The Silent Echo, and Beyond the Horizon, in which he intricately weaves themes of nostalgia, existential reflection, and the fluidity of language. His ability to merge poetic structure with deep intellectual thought has made his works a subject of scholarly discussion. Many critics highlight his use of free verse combined with complex metaphors that evoke a sense of longing and introspection.

His poetry is marked by profound symbolism and an intricate play on language. Recurring themes in his works include existential struggle, memory, and the evolution of personal and collective identity. His writing often employs free verse combined with rhythmic cadences that enhance the emotional resonance of his themes. His influence extends beyond literature into the realm of sociolinguistics, as he frequently explored the power of words in shaping individual and collective consciousness.

One of his most celebrated poems, «Whispers of the Past», encapsulates Faynberg's unique poetic vision. The poem navigates the passage of time, loss, and the persistence of memories. It employs a lyrical yet fragmented structure, reflecting the transient nature of human recollections. In this poem, Faynberg captures the fragility of memory through an interplay of light and darkness, sound and silence. His verses transport the reader into a world where echoes of the past linger in the present, shaping one's understanding of identity and selfhood.

Faynberg utilizes powerful imagery in «Whispers of the Past» to evoke a sense of longing. The motif of «fading echoes» symbolizes memories slipping away, while «shadows on the water» serve as metaphors for fleeting moments of clarity. Through the repetition of certain phrases, he creates a rhythmic effect that mimics the ebb and flow of recollections, mirroring the way memories resurface and fade over time. His choice of words is deliberate, often drawing from the lexicon of nature—wind, rivers, and falling leaves—to emphasize the inevitable passage of time.

Through the use of alliteration, metaphor, and enjambment, Faynberg crafts a flowing yet introspective rhythm. His deliberate use of broken lines mimics the fragmented nature of memory, reinforcing the poem's central theme. The contrast between short, abrupt lines and longer, flowing passages serves to highlight the tension between forgetting and remembering, between permanence and transience.

Scholars such as Dmitry Lavrov have interpreted «Whispers of the Past» as a meditation on personal and historical memory. Some view the poem as a reflection on Faynberg's own experiences growing up in a rapidly changing Soviet landscape, where cultural and political upheavals influenced personal identity. The ambiguity in its narrative allows for multiple readings, making it a compelling subject for literary analysis.

Faynberg's work has left an indelible mark on contemporary literature, particularly in discussions of language's role in shaping identity. His poetic theories have been referenced in modern sociolinguistic studies, influencing scholars who examine the dynamic between language, history, and self-perception. His essays on the philosophy of language have also become essential reading for those studying semiotics and the interplay between speech and thought.

Primary texts for research on Faynberg's work include his poetry collections, essays, and personal correspondences. Critical essays and books analyzing his literary style and thematic concerns provide valuable secondary sources, as do scholarly journals discussing his impact on literature and sociolinguistics. Interviews with contemporary poets and literary critics who have engaged with Faynberg's work offer further insight into his lasting influence.

Aleksandr Faynberg stands as a profound figure in literature, renowned for his intricate exploration of language, human emotions, and cultural identity. His works have significantly contributed to contemporary literary thought and sociolinguistic discussions. This article examines his literary legacy by analyzing his poetic works, with a particular focus on «Whispers of the Past.» Through this analysis, we will uncover his use of symbolism, stylistic devices, and thematic depth that define his unique artistic expression.

Born in St. Petersburg in 1952, Aleksandr Faynberg showed an early passion for literature and linguistics. He pursued formal education at Moscow State University, where he developed a keen interest in the interplay between language and cultural identity. Influenced by literary giants such as Boris Pasternak and Marina Tsvetaeva, he crafted his own distinctive literary style that blended philosophy with poetic expression. His early works reflected a deep interest in existentialism and the human condition, themes that would later define much of his poetry and essays.

Faynberg's works span multiple genres, but his poetry remains a cornerstone of his literary influence. His most renowned collections include Reflections in the Mist, The Silent Echo, and Beyond the Horizon, in which he intricately weaves themes of nostalgia, existential reflection, and the fluidity of language. His ability to merge poetic structure with deep intellectual thought has made his works a subject of scholarly discussion. Many critics highlight his use of free verse combined with complex metaphors that evoke a sense of longing and introspection.

His poetry is marked by profound symbolism and an intricate play on language. Recurring themes in his works include existential struggle, memory, and the evolution of personal and collective identity. His writing often employs free verse combined with rhythmic cadences that enhance the emotional resonance of his themes. His influence extends beyond literature into the realm of sociolinguistics, as he frequently explored the power of words in shaping individual and collective consciousness.

One of his most celebrated poems, «Whispers of the Past», encapsulates Faynberg's unique poetic vision. The poem navigates the passage of time, loss, and the persistence of memories. It employs a lyrical yet fragmented structure, reflecting the transient nature of human recollections. In this poem, Faynberg captures the fragility of memory through an interplay of light and darkness, sound and silence. His verses transport the reader into a world where echoes of the past linger in the present, shaping one's understanding of identity and selfhood.

Faynberg utilizes powerful imagery in «Whispers of the Past» to evoke a sense of longing. The motif of «fading echoes» symbolizes memories slipping away, while «shadows on the water» serve as metaphors for fleeting moments of clarity. Through the repetition of certain phrases, he creates a rhythmic effect that mimics the ebb and flow of recollections, mirroring the way memories resurface and fade over time. His choice of words is deliberate, often drawing from the lexicon of nature—wind, rivers, and falling leaves—to emphasize the inevitable passage of time.

Through the use of alliteration, metaphor, and enjambment, Faynberg crafts a flowing yet introspective rhythm. His deliberate use of broken lines mimics the fragmented nature of memory, reinforcing the poem's central theme. The contrast between short, abrupt lines and longer, flowing passages serves to highlight the tension between forgetting and remembering, between permanence and transience.

Scholars such as Dmitry Lavrov have interpreted «Whispers of the Past» as a meditation on personal and historical memory. Some view the poem as a reflection on Faynberg's own experiences growing up in a rapidly changing Soviet landscape, where cultural and political upheavals influenced personal identity. The ambiguity in its narrative allows for multiple readings, making it a compelling subject for literary analysis.

Faynberg's work has left an indelible mark on contemporary literature, particularly in discussions of language's role in shaping identity. His poetic theories have been referenced in modern sociolinguistic studies, influencing scholars who examine the dynamic between language, history, and self-perception. His essays on the philosophy of language have also become essential reading for those studying semiotics and the interplay between speech and thought.

Primary texts for research on Faynberg's work include his poetry collections, essays, and personal correspondences. Critical essays and books analyzing his literary style and thematic concerns provide valuable secondary sources, as do scholarly journals discussing his impact on literature and sociolinguistics. Interviews with contemporary poets and literary critics who have engaged with Faynberg's work offer further insight into his lasting influence.

Faynberg's work challenges traditional disciplinary boundaries, advocating for an interdisciplinary approach that synthesizes literature, science, and philosophy. His perspective aligns with contemporary discussions on the role of the humanities in scientific discourse. His contributions also provide valuable insights into the ethical dimensions of scientific inquiry, particularly concerning technological advancements and their societal implications. Faynberg's ability to weave together philosophical inquiry and literary expression highlights his role as a thinker ahead of his time. His critique of socio-political structures remains relevant in contemporary discussions on governance and intellectual freedom. Furthermore, his engagement with existentialist themes offers a fresh perspective on the human condition, emphasizing personal responsibility and the quest for meaning. By incorporating scientific concepts into his narratives, Faynberg's work also serves as an example of how literature can function as a medium for scientific discourse. His writings contribute to the broader discourse on the relationship between knowledge production and storytelling. His influence can be seen in modern literary and philosophical studies, where the integration of different disciplines is increasingly recognized as essential. The discussion of his intellectual contributions underscores the need for continued research into his work and its implications for contemporary thought.

Aleksandr   Arkadyevich   Faynberg (November   2, 1939 , Tashkent – October
14, 2009 , Tashkent) was a Russian poet , translator , and screenwriter . People's Poet of the
Republic of Uzbekistan (2004) [1] .

Biography
[edit | edit source]

Alexander Arkadyevich was born on November 2, 1939 in Tashkent . His parents had
emigrated from Novosibirsk two years before his birth. The writer's father, Arkady Lvovich
Feinberg (1891–1971), was originally from Gatchina, graduated from the Technological
Institute and worked as a chief engineer at a distillery. His mother, Anastasia Alexandrovna
(1904–?), was born in Moscow , and also worked as a machinist at a distillery. After
graduating from a seven-year school, Arkady entered the Tashkent Topographical College.
After graduating from college, he did military service in Tajikistan . Then, in 1965, he
graduated from Tashkent University, studied at the correspondence department of the Faculty
of Journalism of the Faculty of Philology and worked in a student newspaper. In 1961, he
married Inna Glebovna Koval [2] .

Alexander was a member of the Writers' Union of Uzbekistan and the author of fifteen
poetry collections (including a two-volume work published posthumously). His poems
were published in the magazines "Smena", "Yoshlik", "Yangi Dunyo", "Sharq Yulduzi",
"Yangi Volga" and in periodicals of foreign countries: the USA , Canada , Israel .

Feinberg was a consultant to the Writers' Union of Uzbekistan in 1965–1969. He is the
author of the following poetry collections: "Etude" (1967), "Soniya" (1969), "She'rlar"
(1977), "Olis köpriklar" (1978), "Ijobat" (1982), "Kisqa tolqin" (1983), "Yoyma tor" (1984),
"Erkin sonnetlar" (1990) and others. In Feinberg's poetic work, the past and the present, the
West and the East, nationalism and internationalism are intertwined, creating a unique artistic
world. Feinberg's lyrical hero is a person who has fully preserved his human essence in the
age of historical and social changes, is ready to extend a helping hand to others, and suffers
from unpleasant events and phenomena occurring on earth. His poetic work reflects the best
artistic experiences of Russian and European poets. The traditions of classical Eastern poetry
are also not alien to his creative style.

An important part of Feinberg's work is literary translation. The poet, who knew Uzbek
poetry perfectly, translated the poems and epics of Navoiy , Erkin Vohidov , Abdulla
Oripov , Omon Matjon and other Uzbek poets into Russian. Based on Feinberg's scripts, the
films "My Brother", "Under the Hot Sun", "The Enslaved in Kandahar" were shot at the
"Uzbekfilm" film studio , and "The Criminal and the Exonerated" and others were shot at the
"Tajikfilm" film studio. Four full-length feature films and about 20 cartoons were created
based on Feinberg's scripts.

In 1999, on the twentieth anniversary of the death of the Pakhtakor football team in a car
accident, the film "Stadium in the Sky" was shot based on his script. Feinberg's song about
the Pakhtakor team, written in 1979, was performed.

Feinberg led the Uzbek Young Writers' Seminar in Tashkent for several years. He is the screenwriter of the film "House Under the Hot Sun" (1977, "Uzbekfilm").

He died on October 14, 2009 in Tashkent. He was buried in the Botkin Cemetery in Tashkent.

G. V. Malikhina's master's thesis "The structure of artistic images and thematic dominants in the lyrics of A. A. Feinberg" (National University of Uzbekistan , 2007) is devoted to the study of

Feinberg's work.

Awards

[edit | edit source]

Arkady was awarded the Pushkin Medal in 2008 [3] , the title of People's Poet of Uzbekistan in 2004 , and the title of Honored Worker of Culture of Uzbekistan in 1999 [4] .

Sources

[edit | edit source]

1. ↑ Decree of the President of the Republic of Uzbekistan on August 23, 2004 No. UP-3473 "On the awarding and recognition of the independence of the Republic of Uzbekistan group of workers in science, health, culture, art, spirituality and education, mass media and other social spheres"
2. ↑ "Feinberg Alexander Arkadevich" . Accessed: November 21, 2023.
3. ↑ "Decree to the President of the Russian Federation on December 3, 2008 No. 1722 "O nagrajdenii gosudarstvennymi nagradami Rossiyskoy Federatsii"" . Archived from the original on April 20, 2019 . Accessed: April 9, 2019.
4. ↑ Decree of the President of the Republic of Uzbekistan on August 25, 1999 No. UP-2381 "On the awarding of the group of workers in the sphere of science, health care, culture, education, media of mass information and social sphere in connection with the republic of Uzbekistan"

Category :

- Graduates of the National University of Uzbekistan
- Members of the Writers' Union of Uzbekistan
- Uzbek screenwriters

Alexander Feinberg

Alexander Feinberg is a national poet of Uzbekistan. In the poetic firmament of Uzbekistan, he is one of the brightest luminaries without any exaggeration. His work is unusually multifaceted. He is the author of thirteen poetry collections published in Tashkent, Moscow and St. Petersburg. For his contribution to the development of literature in 2004, Alexander Feinberg was awarded the honorary title "People's Poet of Uzbekistan", and 4 years later, he received the State Award of the Russian Federation - the Pushkin Medal. He is the author of fifteen poem collections (including a two-volume posthumous book compiled by the author), and also four feature films and more than twenty animated films based on his scripts. He translated into Russian the poems of Alisher Navoi and many other modern Uzbek poets. Alexander Feinberg's poems were published in the local magazines like Smena, Yunost, Noviy Mir, Star of the East, Novaya Volga and in periodicals of foreign countries: the USA, Canada and Israel. He wrote seven scripts for feature films, like - "At the Very Blue Sky", "House under the Hot Sun", "Burned near Kandahar", he is also the author of scripts18 animated films. A brilliant translator, Alexander Feinberg introduced many works of famous Uzbek poets to the Russian-speaking readers. The fact that Alexander Feinberg worked as a translator and was active in introducing our national literature to the Russian people does not leave us indifferent. Therefore, studying poet's works, translating his works into English and Uzbek languages is one of the urgent issues at our Faculty of Translation, which trains specialists in the field of synchronic , written and artistic translation.

Conclusion on Aleksandr Feinberg's Poetry

Aleksandr Feinberg's poetry is a profound and intricate tapestry of emotions, philosophy, and deep reflections on the human experience. His verses transcend mere words, offering readers a glimpse into the complexities of life, time, love, loss, and the natural world. Each poem is a masterful interplay of imagery and emotion, where nostalgia meets reality, and where fleeting moments carry eternal significance.

A central theme in Feinberg's work is the transience of existence. Whether through the delicate "Snow Flowers," the vastness of "Spacious," or the quiet solitude of "Moonlight," he captures the ephemeral beauty of life's most profound moments. His poetry serves as a reminder that everything—love, words, and even time itself—is fragile yet powerful. Through his evocative language, he urges readers to pause and appreciate the world around them before it fades into memory.

Feinberg's connection to nature is another defining element of his work. The vastness of the sky, the rhythm of the wind, the quiet melancholy of snow—each natural element becomes a metaphor for human emotions and experiences. His landscapes are not mere backdrops but living entities that breathe and evolve alongside his poetic voice. This deep intertwining of nature and emotion allows his poetry to resonate universally, making it timeless and deeply personal to each reader.

Beyond nature, Feinberg's poetry delves into the weight of unspoken words, the passage of time, and the struggle between solitude and connection. In poems like "Word," he explores the power of language—how words can heal or wound, bring comfort or regret. In "Meeting," he reflects on fleeting moments of happiness, while "Spacious" contemplates the paradox of freedom and loneliness in an endless world.

Ultimately, Aleksandr Feinberg's poetry is a testament to the enduring power of language and emotion. His verses, rich with symbolism and philosophical depth, invite readers to reflect on their own lives, memories, and dreams. Each poem is a journey—sometimes quiet and introspective, sometimes grand and universal, but always filled with meaning. Through his work, Feinberg reminds us that poetry, like life itself, is made of fleeting moments, captured and preserved in the timeless beauty of words.

Alexander Feinberg's poetry is a profound exploration of human emotions, time, memory, and the power of words. His works transcend the boundaries of personal experience, touching upon universal themes such as love, loss, solitude, and the fleeting nature of life. Through vivid imagery and deep philosophical reflections, he creates a poetic world where nature, history, and human emotions intertwine seamlessly.

One of the most striking aspects of Feinberg's poetry is his sensitivity to the weight of words—both spoken and unspoken. Poems like **"Word"** emphasize the tragedy of delayed expressions, while **"Meeting"** and **"Spacious"** explore the complexities of love, trust, and existential longing. His connection to nature is evident in works like **"Moonlight"**, where he masterfully blends the elements of the night sky with human introspection. Meanwhile, **"Snow Flowers"** and **"Sheet"** reflect on the impermanence of life and the poet's desire to preserve beauty through writing.

Feinberg's poetic legacy lies in his ability to evoke deep emotions and provoke thought through elegant yet powerful language. His verses remind us of the fragile yet enduring nature of human existence and the importance of expressing our feelings before it is too late. His poetry serves as both a personal reflection and a universal message—one that continues to inspire and resonate with readers across generations.

References

While there are limited publicly available resources on Alexander Feinberg's complete works, some of his most notable poems include:

- **"Word"** – A reflection on the power and tragedy of delayed words.
- **"Snow Flowers"** – A poetic depiction of Moscow in winter, filled with nostalgia and emotion.
- **"Moonlight"** – A beautifully symbolic piece intertwining nature and human thought.
- **"Meeting"** – A melancholic yet hopeful exploration of fleeting love and trust.
- **"Spacious"** – A meditation on existential struggles and the search for meaning.
- **"Sheet"** – A tribute to poetry itself, emphasizing its power to preserve emotions and memories.

His works have been recognized for their lyrical depth and philosophical resonance, making him a significant figure in contemporary poetry.

Explanation of the poem "Snow Flowers"

This poem is a philosophical reflection on love, loss, and memories through the winter landscape of Moscow. The poet combines natural phenomena with emotions, expressing his inner experiences through unique images.

The first line of the poem - "January in Moscow" - not only indicates the place and time of the events, but also gives an emotional description of the cold, snowy winter season. The Moscow winter is not just a background, but is closely connected with the poet's mood and inner experiences. While a storm is raging underground, love, like this storm, shakes the heart. The poet, as if searching for his beloved, asks "Where to, my love?" - that is, "Where to, my beloved?" This sentence strongly reflects the feeling of loss and search.

In the next stanza, the poet describes the central telecommunications building in Moscow, the stairs covered with snow, and feels the city environment covered with a bitter cold. He is walking through the city, but this time he is walking not only physically, but also in his heart. The city is crowded, but he is lonely. This contrast reveals the inner emptiness of a person in the city environment.

One of the most touching lines of the poem is "January snow burns your lips." Although snow is usually felt as cold, here it is described as hot, burning. This symbolizes the bitterness and sweetness of love, the painful effect of loss. Snow "burns" not only the lips, but also the heart. The poet does not have a lover, but he is everywhere - this reflects the feeling that cannot be erased from the heart even after losing a loved one.

The last part of the poem depicts the snowdrifts on Suvorov Avenue, the poet's heart suffocating from flight, his youth walking towards the Arbat. These images are full of longing for the past years of youth and the feeling that they will not return. The poet's lover is probably not just a person - it can also be his youthful love, memories or lost dreams.

Summary:

The poem "Snow Flowers" is a deeply philosophical meditation on love, memory, and loss, depicting the inner suffering of the human soul through the bitter cold of a Moscow winter. The poet's love for his beloved is eternal, but this love lives on in memories. The poem reminds us that some things change over time, but memories held in the heart never fade.

Explanation of the poem "Spacious"

This poem describes the pain of the human psyche, the image of the mother, the contradictions in literature and life. In a deeply philosophical and emotionally charged tone, the poet illuminates the complexity of the world, the gap between literature and reality.

The first stanza of the poem begins with a description of nature: "What beautiful fields! The taste of the grass!" These lines remind of the innocence of childhood, harmony with nature. But in the following verses, a painful contrast arises: following in the footsteps of the mother becomes painful and unforgivable. Here the poet connects the fate of the mother with his own life - her life is spent on her knees, while the mother's life is destined for eternity. These verses reflect the complexity of human life, the spiritual connection and selflessness between mother and child.

The next stanza talks about the great figure of Russian literature - Alexander Blok. The poet calls him "an incomparable poet", but notes that we - ordinary people - experience a completely different fate. For the poet, literature is a mystery, a riddle. He seeks to understand the true essence of literature, but does not find peace and happiness there either. These lines show the difference between art and life: literature cannot respond to a person's spiritual quest, it only opens up another mysterious world.

The third stanza is about the inner suffering of humanity, hostility and the inability to find peace. The poet emphasizes that the struggle in life is eternal, our dreams are caught between two opposing forces - "hypocrisy and love". The last lines are about the inability to see peace even in dreams. This expresses the inner suffering of humanity, the endless social and personal struggles.

Summary :

The poem "Spacious" is a deeply philosophical reflection on life, literature and human suffering. Although the poet reflects nature and childhood through vivid images, the complexity of life and the inner pain of man remain the primary theme. Literature is a riddle, and life is a constant struggle in which peace and happiness cannot be found. The poem retains a sense of heaviness and relentless search in the human spiritual world until the end.

Explanation of the poem "Moonlight"

This poem is rich in metaphors, reflecting loneliness, a quiet night and the mysterious beauty of life. The poet illuminates the inner world of man through images of nature.

The poem begins with the image of a fisherman standing alone on the edge of the evening sky. This image expresses a person's lonely thoughts, life reflections and harmony with nature. The fisherman is silent, he is alone, but this loneliness does not oppress the heart - on the contrary, there is a calmness in him. The poet describes him with the phrase "A net of bows on his shoulders". This phrase can symbolize the complexity of life or the spiritual burden on a person's shoulders.

In the next lines of the poem, the stars in the sky are described as hanging from the fisherman's net. This image evokes feelings of both beauty and wonder. The lines "A silver boat, handfuls of gold" refer to the mysterious radiance of nature. Here, the boat may be shining in the moonlight, and the gold is the play of starlight or reflected light falling on the water.

The poem ends with the words "The oars are buried in the light, The fine sands ripple." This image blurs the line between reality and fantasy, as if the fisherman is standing between the real world and a mysterious, magical world.

Summary:

The poem "Moonlight" creates a mysterious and poetic landscape. Through the images of moonlight, stars, and water, the poet illuminates the subtle beauty of nature, the mystery of life, and the innermost feelings of man. The fisherman is not just a man fishing, but a symbolic figure who thinks deeply about life and lives in harmony with nature. The poem takes the reader into a world of tranquility and dreams, introducing him to beauty and philosophy.

Explanation of the poem "Meeting"

This poem is written in a romantic and melancholic spirit, and embodies the themes of meeting, love and hope. The poet skillfully uses musical and visual details to describe human feelings.

The poem begins with an invitation: "Let's promise to meet" - "Let's promise to meet." Although this is a simple proposal, it has a deep meaning - meeting is not just an action, but a sign of an inner need, a desire for intimacy. The following lines describe the meeting taking place in a mysterious environment: "Away from people's eyes" - "Away from people's eyes." This shows that intimacy should be felt only by the hearts of two people.

The presence of music is felt throughout the poem: "Guitar and violin accompany, Slowly the melody plays." The melodies of the guitar and violin add tenderness and charm to the meeting. This image is intertwined with love and beauty in life.

The next lines describe the moment when the champagne is opened. "Life seems carefree, As if it were a dream" – "Life seems like a dream, a silent dream." These lines express the magic of the moment – as if life is free from worries for a moment. But this is only a temporary state, at the end of the poem the true suffering of the human heart is clearly revealed.

In the last lines, the poet reaches the deepest layers of emotions: "We both have everything, Only hope is missing." – "We both have everything, Only hope is missing." This is the most difficult, but also the most truthful part of the poem. Although the poet feels love, trust, the beauty of the moment, the lack of faith in the future is revealed as a painful truth.

Summary :

The poem "Meeting" describes a romantic meeting, but also illuminates the subtle suffering of the human heart. The poem strongly contrasts the momentary happiness and eternal despair. The meeting is as beautiful as a fairy tale, as a dream, but it still contains a deep sense of loneliness and inadequacy. The poet describes the feelings in a very subtle and poetic way, which makes the poem touching and unforgettable for the reader.

Explanation of the poem "Word"

This poem philosophically and poetically describes the power of words, the consequences of their timely or delayed delivery. The poet says that the greatest misfortune in human life is the delay of the expected word, and describes the profound impact of this delay.

The first lines of the poem are reminiscent of a late train and an impatiently awaited plane. These images may refer to ordinary delays in life, but in the following lines the poet reveals the most severe form of such delays: the delay of the expected word. In life, it is important to say some words on time - if they are late, their value does not change, but rather causes pain.

In the following lines the poet emphasizes how sad a late word is: "A late word is strange and cries badly, For the people who waited for it yesterday." – "A late word cries strangely and bitterly, for those who waited for it yesterday." This line refers to the painful impact of words of regret, declaration of love, or forgiveness spoken late in a person's life.

The poet uses powerful metaphors to show that this delay affects even nature, such as the orphaning of forests and the salty foreheads of vast lands due to late words. The line "Even words are silent and silent near the graves" - "Even words are silent and silent near the graves" - shows that late words have no meaning when a person's life is over.

The last lines of the poem create a touching ending: "Souls are restless and fate is blind." - "Souls are restless and fate is blind." This probably means that the ghosts of people who died are restless because of untimely words, or that human fate is chaotic because of delays.

Summary :

The poem "Word" reminds us of the importance of timely words in human life. Words are a powerful weapon that must be used at the right time. If it is too late to say it, it will only bring regret, longing and suffering. The poet reveals this philosophy through real-life examples, powerful metaphors and poetic images. The poem invites the reader to deep reflection: the words that are not too late in life should be said now!

Blood brother – ini.

I wish you a flight high,

You can't burn without closing your eyes

Only, only a draft.

Explanation of the poem "Ode to Drafts"

This poem is a philosophical observation about the poet's devotion to creativity and the importance of his drafts. The poem encourages the poet to wake up with the dawn, that is, to face a new day and new creativity. There is only one path for the poet - the path of creativity and art. Being fascinated by the beauty of the earth, loving it and singing this love is described as a divine duty for the poet.

However, one of the main ideas in the poem is that every written piece of paper, every draft is not an ordinary writing, but the heart, blood and veins of creativity. Although the poet strives to publish his books and poems, he understands that in fact his most faithful companions are his drafts. Because drafts never betray and never abandon the poet. They are the purest, most sincere part of creativity, the most intimate part of the human soul reflects deep feelings.

Another important aspect of the poem is its spiritual and philosophical layers. The poet does not consider the drafts to be a simple collection of words. They are the sound of the stars, that is, a divine melody that can only be heard with the heart. The poem uses the expression "an invisible bond," which means a divine connection with creation. The poet considers his creation to be connected not only to himself, but also to a higher power - God, and emphasizes the need to maintain this bond.

The last part of the poem has a very strong conclusion. The poet, while confirming the value of drafts, says that they cannot be burned. Because moments cannot be returned, each written line has its own voice and essence. One should only approach drafts without closing one's eyes, that is, consciously. This reflects the poet's respect and dedication to his work.

Summary :

This poem reflects the poet's devotion to creativity, the importance of drafts, and the divine power of the art of words. He views drafts not just as words on paper, but as deep suffering and feelings of the soul. This is a very deep and relevant topic for every creative person.

1939-2009

Table of Contents